DARTMOOR

in the

OLD DAYS

James Mildren

BOSSINEY BOOKS

First published in 1984
by Bossiney Books
St Teath, Bodmin, Cornwall.
Designed, printed and bound in Great Britain by
A. Wheaton & Co. Ltd, Exeter.

ISBN 0 906456 89 4

Front cover: The miller's cart, Widecombe, 1890.
Back cover: The Reverend W.A. Gray, Rector of Meavy,
supervises the raising of stones at Down Tor in 1895.

ABOUT THE AUTHOR – AND THE BOOK

James Mildren lived at Tavistock for twenty years – in *My Devon*, published by Bossiney Books, he described it as '... an almost perfect place'. He now resides in Devonport. As a journalist he has worked first on the *Tavistock Gazette*, and then in 1967 he joined *The Western Morning News* where he has been Environment Correspondent since 1971, except for a short spell as Regional Information Officer with The National Trust in Cornwall.

James Mildren is an author who is at home in the wilderness of his Dartmoor. His words and a magnificent collection of old photographs unite to produce an evocative portrait of this lovely yet alien landscape.

'These photographs', he says, 'will arouse in many people a deep sense of nostalgia, fond remembrances, perhaps, of the days that are no more. To me, they are but a tiny fragment of the vast evolution of a place which – as a man of Devon – I have come to adore.'

DARTMOOR IN THE OLD DAYS

Many of these photographs belong to the Victorian era, and it occurs to me that it is very much due to that Queen's love of solitude that such wildernesses as Dartmoor became fashionable.

Those who believe the theory is far-fetched should, for instance, examine the clothes worn by the women of the time. Glance, for example, overleaf at the wonderful poise – and dress – of Rebecca Finch and her family at Sticklepath.

Does she not epitomise what we have come to loosely describe as the best in Victorian values?

I find it odd that Queen Victoria never appears to have set foot on Dartmoor itself. Wearing her mourning like a millstone, she retreated to Deeside and, in doing so, set an example to her countrymen and women.

Read her journals – as the Victorians did – and it becomes clear its very wilderness acted upon the Royal person like a tonic.

Sketching, fishing, pony trekking, or just travelling in her carriage across the lonely moorland, helped heal her inner torment, and appeared to endow her with the strength to continue her exalted duties.

Above: Bowerman's Nose: 'All seemed to breathe freedom and
peace, and to make one forget the world and its sad turmoils.'

Left: Toppers, boaters and handsome bowlers: this nattily-dressed
party – members of the Plymouth Athenaeum – has excursed
towards Tavy Cleave upon a July day in 1891. This photograph
was taken by Robert Burnard, grandfather of Lady Sayer.

Memorable are the views from Kes Tor. The railings behind the figure on top of the rock were placed there in the mid-nineteenth century by G. W. Ormerod of Chagford who unchoked one of the largest rock basins ever discovered in such a situation on the Moor. This picture postcard view was taken around 1912.

Chagford market-place

And I cannot but muse on the possibility that had she indeed chosen Dartmoor, rather than Scotland, Victoria would have found here the stress-relieving solitude, the wonderful silence and the compassionate appealing countenance which she happily discovered in the northern reaches of her Island domain.

If it was good enough for the Queen – and right for her – then why, her subjects were entitled to ask, shouldn't it be good enough for everybody?

Was it merely by accident that so many of the great amenity groups began their existence in her reign – the Commons and Open Spaces Society, for instance; The National Trust, which has grown, subsequently, into the largest conservation body of its kind to be found anywhere; and, not least, the Dartmoor Preservation Association, founded in 1883.

Dartmoor, an upland sea of granite, was itself beginning to emerge from a dreamlike state at the end of Victoria's reign.

The last real attempt by a mere man to pit himself against this monolithic Moor had been made by Thomas Tyrwhitt, a friend of the Prince Regent, who had the temerity to scratch Dartmoor's back: he obtained the usual reward for such folly – it split his purse!

Only Dartmoor Prison among his would-be

works of creation managed to survive as a reminder to our generation of his vain struggle to conquer Nature. And Dartmoor Prison itself will go, sooner or later.

Many others have battled against this great Moor – tinners, farmers, flockmasters and roadmakers. Their memorials are contained in the humour of the soil, scars on the kaleidoscope of this often baleful-looking, but revered and ancient landscape.

As fickle a mistress as ever she was, many would-be conquerers gaze longingly at the wide, inviting acres, so many of them like the

purblind Argus – all eyes, and no sight.

Dartmoor, infinite in mood, scarred with use, will not lightly remit its character to those who would challenge solitude.

To understand it is to love it – and Dartmoor does seem to respond with something approaching affection to those who make of this Moor a partner rather than prisoner.

The long and clamorous bray of developers blasts against the winds which roam the lonely eminences and the places where the hoary dew melts slowly into flashing rivers. This Moor gulphs time itself.

There is no easy bounty from this mighty backbone of Devon to be won without due measure.

Tin was panned out sparingly; few farmers have been able to scratch out much more than a thin living from the peaty, acid soil, scarcely deep enough to bury their dead.

The Finches of Sticklepath. Rebecca, with the poise of a matriarch, and eyes as bright as the cutting edge of the superbly manufactured tools in the old foundry – which existed from 1814 to 1960 – is surrounded by her flock.

Sombre a place it often is, but lacking in interest, never.

When these old photographs began to be taken, there were ominous signs that Tyrwhitt's attempts to tame this granite-boned giant were to be revived.

The prison had been opened; the military occupation had begun – initially, it should be noted, without any compensation being paid to the commoners of Dartmoor for their loss of rights.

Land was being enclosed, especially on the fringes of the moorland; china clay had been found, and was being worked out in some places – at Redlake, for instance.

The manufacturers of that strange new power source, electricity, were looking to the hills – not for comfort or salvation – but for river sources; the need for more water supplies for domestic and industrial purposes was becoming paramount – and Dartmoor was seen, even, as a fir-clad forest yielding untold tonnes of timber.

Ironic as it must have seemed to those would-be developers, a powerful counter-balancing force began to spring up almost simultaneously. The scales may have been weighted heavily against them, in material terms, ever since, but their fight has been unremitting to save Dartmoor from unnecessary spoilation.

Men and women, interested in Dartmoor for its archaeological, historical and natural scientific treasures, argued with great persuasive power, that these facets were no less valuable to man than the work ethic itself.

While James Bryce, Octavia Hill and like-minded men and women fought for the conservation ethic, the Dartmoor Preservation Association came into being and, for a hundred years now, has pointed an admonitory finger accusingly at the speculators and the predators.

Amazingly, a wholly unanticipated ally lay at their finger-tips – the camera!

Splendid though the prose of the time undoubtedly was, it was as much a truism then as it is to this day that one picture is worth a thousand words.

Again, it was an era of cheap and efficient postal services, a time when the postcard was a most popular form of instant communication – long before the wearisome telephone.

Printing, also, was enjoying a golden age.

Thanks to a felicitous combination of communications, with the emphasis as much on the visual as the verbal, the message about Dartmoor began to leak out to the wider world.

There were also some very remarkable people living at that time. Sabine Baring-Gould, for example, whose preservation instinct was (thankfully) almost obsessive a pre-occupation; Robert Burnard, an amateur photographer of outstanding ability, whose grand-daughter, Lady Sayer, has become synonymous with the cause of conservation in this half of the twentieth century.

Nor should we overlook such deeply committed men as Harry Price, the young sailor, whose love affair with Fingle Bridge is one of the most romantic tales ever to emerge from the Moor.

Yet another huge contribution to Dartmoor's cause was provided by William Crossing, whose 1909 Guide ranks, perhaps, second only to William Wordsworth's classic book about the Lake District. What a debt we owe to the poverty-haunted Crossing!

Not until this half of the twentieth century with the appearance of Worth's *Dartmoor* (1953) and, in this very decade, Eric Hemery's *High Dartmoor* (1983) was Crossing's output to be matched.

In addition, an increasing number of fine artists began to take their inspiration from the Moor – Frederick John Widgery, William Cook, F.J. Snell and the Brittains, father and son.

And who can erase the work of Eden Phillpotts, surely a writer whose novels are only temporarily neglected?

Already, of course, Wordsworth had boldly suggested that his district (The Lakes) should

Right: A more enchanting scene it would be hard to imagine than the simple rusticity of Lustleigh, long before the invasion of the motorcar.

Luncheon on the banks of the River Teign.
Another of Robert Burnard's photographs.

be made 'a sort of national property in which
every man has an interest who has an eye to
perceive or a heart to rejoice'.

Burnard, and others, shared that vision – for
Dartmoor. Not until 1951, however, was it to be
designated as a national park.

Yet, sadly, for as long as tycoons dictate
national interests, wilderness will never be safe.
Solitude is not yet regarded as a national
resource, primarily because it cannot be cost-
accounted.

These old photographs will arouse in many
people a deep sense of nostalgia, fond
remembrances, perhaps, of the days that are no
more.

To me, they are but a tiny fragment of the vast
evolution of a place which – as a man of Devon –
I have come to adore.

History has shown that Dartmoor has

endured all that man has so far flung at it: what
a long love-hate relationship it has already
been.

Significantly, it has outlived friend and foe
alike.

I cannot pass by Crockern Tor, for example,
without thinking of the tin despots, that
turbulent assembly of miners who believed
themselves, in the freemasonry of their *al fresco*
Stannary Courts, to be above the law of the land
itself. They were confounded by the nobly
rebellious Dick Strode, MP for Plympton, who
dared put them in their place.

What pomp and pageantry there was, too, in
the Benedictine Abbey of Tavistock, whose
mitred Abbot looked, in the Abbey's last days,
to Rome for his orders, and not to Westminster
or Exeter.

The canonical hours, the chanted matins are
no more – the Lady Chapel and its reliquaries
lie buried beneath four feet of roadway.

Many times have I paused on Dartmoor of a
Spring evening, when the air is clear as wine
and chill breezes shake the catkins and numb

the shivering lambs, and imagined I heard a Sanctus Bell: yet it was merely the ring of laughter from children in streams nearby.

Oh what a fall was there at the disestablishment of those ecclesiastical fortresses!

In the silence of a winter's day, when clouds of snow-threatening density gather on the eastern rim of this mighty place, the landscape conjures up the desolation of a Sibelius symphony.

Or, in the rich garb of autumn, when the russet-coloured bracken garlands in dead fronds the cracked and weathered prehistoric remains, the harmonies of the season are as magical as a Wagnerian melody or as profound and moving as some sublime adagio of Beethoven.

At Holy Street Mill, Chagford: 'To understand Dartmoor is to love it.'

Often, this scene of vastness and of echo, permeated with a heavy and lingering aroma of the past, will drench the listener, the onlooker, in a torrent of penetrating rain or mist.

The public enters Dartmoor at its own risk of weather!

Always, it seems, there are buzzards or kestrels in sight, joyriding on the thermals, volplaning over the tors.

Invariably, though, I am conscious of being no more than a marginal entry upon the densely-layered palimpsest of this ancient creature which we call Dartmoor.

These old photographs mirror the work of others, who have made a more permanent mark: I hope you may share some of my joy in them.

Has so much changed in the 140 years, or so, since Queen Victoria herself wrote, on her very first visit to Deeside:

'All seemed to breathe freedom and peace, and to make one forget the world and its sad turmoils.'

Tavistock is one of the gateway towns to Dartmoor.
These old postcards, despatched in 1905, are indicative of just
how little Tavistock, among the loveliest of all British towns, has
changed.

The railings around St Eustachius Church (*below right*) have
gone, part of the war effort, and the discreet gas-lamp standards
have been replaced by other street furniture which is both ugly
and intrusive.

The tall spire of the former Congregational Church seen behind
the forest of pinnacles surrounding the Guildhall Square (*above*)
has been demolished, and the square itself has become a carpark.
One day, perhaps, Tavistock may pedestrianise the area around
this group of glorious Hurdwick stone buildings, never intended
to be dominated by a steely plinth of motor vehicles.

Mercifully, the Abbey Bridge (*above right*) is unscathed, and
salmon can still find their way up the fast-flowing Tavy to the
clear, still pools at the foot of Dartmoor's tors.

Barely discernible on his rounded granite plinth in Guildhall
Square (*above*), Francis, Duke of Bedford, gazes with statuary
impassiveness down the Plymouth Road towards the statue of
Tavistock's famous son, Francis Drake.

The Bedfords were granted Tavistock Abbey and its lands by
King Henry VIII at the dissolution of the monasteries in 1539.

The ivy-covered Abbey Gateway was one of the original four
entrances to the great Benedictine Abbey.

The Abbots have gone: the Bedfords, having created much of
present-day Tavistock from the huge royalties received from the
156 mines hereabouts, now prefer Woburn to Tavistock.

Left: The Church of St Michael, Brentor, north of Tavistock, commands wonderful views to those prepared to trudge up the steep slopes of this volcanic outcrop.

'A church full bleak and weatherbeaten' said one Devon scribe of this place, 'all alone, as if forsaken, whose churchyard doth hardly afford depth of earth to bury the dead: yet doubtless they rest there as securely as in sumptuous St Peter's, until the day of doom!'

Above: Peeping coyly above the distant horizon is yet another church dedicated to St Michael. This time in Princetown. It is the only one in the world, or so it is said, to have been built and fitted completely by prisoners of war (1813).

It contains a memorial to Sir Thomas Tyrwhitt, a Regency Warden of the Stannaries, who strove to populate Dartmoor's barren wastes with only limited success. There is also an east window dedicated by the Daughters of the American Revolution, who make periodic visits to Princetown.

Parcere Subjectis – Spare the Vanquished – reads the sign over
the main gateway to Number Seven, Tor View, Princetown –
the postal address of one of the world's most infamous retreats.
The photograph of the entrance (*right*) taken in Victorian times
is reversed – see the initials VR above the notice.

Then, as now, Dartmoor Prison had a macabre fascination,
attracting visitors from far and near. Built originally to house
thousands of French – and, later, American – prisoners of war at
the beginning of the nineteenth century, the prison began its
life as a British penal reform establishment in the 1850s.

The catalogue of crime which has resulted in the incarceration
of thousands behind these walls reads like a litany of horror.
Few managed to permanently escape its clutches.

Harnessed like mules, these beasts of burden (*above*) are
Dartmoor prisoners at the beginning of this century. Flogging,
strait-jackets, leg-irons, 'solitary', bread and water diets and
even the ball and chain were then the kind of punishments meted
out to any who dared disobey prison rules. The prison was, at
that time, described, with some justification, as being 'Halfway
to Hell'.

Guards are no longer armed, as they were in Victoria's day,
nor are prisoners harnessed like horses to haul loads through
the streets of Princetown.

Conditions inside are no longer as severe as those which
prompted the riot of 1932, and a new class of inmate, usually
from the region, has largely replaced the former occupants –
men whose offences shocked society.

Dartmoor's weather is notoriously fickle. The winters of 1947 and 1962-3 rank high among the worst remembered on the Moor. But nothing, not even the winter of '47, or the never-ending ice of '62-3 matches the memory of the Great Blizzard of 9 March 1891.

It raged for 36 hours, and the snow lay on the hill country until May. That blizzard acquired legendary fame, although it may have been in many respects no worse than those which swept Dartmoor in 1881, 1886 and again in 1929.

In places, the snow was seven feet deep, in others, it had drifted to Baron Munchausen levels. The moorland farmers have heavy losses to face at such times.

Firmly trapped in the Snow King's grip in these photographs (*below and right*) in 1891 is the Princetown 'express'. The line has long since disappeared, but the memories linger on.

The tang of a 'yaffle o' peat' caught up in a blazing faggot of crackling furze was, Frank Booker reminds us, once a characteristic smell on Dartmoor. The 'vags' being cut here in 1913 by a triangular budding iron from a 'tie' of peat, took the place of coal for local people.

If ancient accounts are at all reliable, suggests the naturalist, Douglas Gordon, then badgers were practically unknown upon the Devonshire highlands a hundred years ago.

But 'grayes', as these creatures were once known, were numerous in the wooded coombes which mark the course of the Dartmoor rivers to the lowlands; hence Badger's Holt, caught in the tranquillity of an evening in July in 1889 by Robert Burnard.

William Crossing makes no mention of it in his *Guide*, and it is left to Eric Hemery, whose splendid volume, *High Dartmoor* (Robert Hale, 1983), is the late-twentieth-century's major contribution to the literature of the Moor, to recall, through an article which appeared in the London *Times* , the journeyings of a Dartmoor roundsman.

This was a time, as Mr Hemery reminds us through that feature, when residents on the Moor sat in the dimpsey, the long Dartmoor twilight, without television or radio or any of the cornucopia of electrical intelligence, until the oil lamps were lit, to illumine the gloom and, perhaps, interrupt the solemn self-imposed silence.

Looking up to Badger's Holt from Dartmeet, the heart of
Dartmoor, as popular in the past for a picnic as it is today.

Huccaby House, 1909, home of the Burnard family, and Mecca for those involved in the developing fascination with the archaeological treasures of the Moor. The house was acquired by Charles Burnard, a founder member of the Dartmoor Preservation Association (1883) who was head of the family business in Plymouth. It was during the construction of deep-water wharves at Cattedown, Plymouth, that his son, Robert, developed what was to become a life-long interest in antiquities.

Robert Burnard (1848-1920). A gifted amateur photographer who combined his love of moorland antiquities with a rare eye for its general character and its inhabitants. He was the first man to propose a solution to Dartmoor's conservation problem by suggesting a national-park-style solution: interestingly, 40 years were to elapse before, in 1951, Burnard's dreams were to become reality. During his life, he was elected a Fellow of the Society of Antiquaries, President of the Devonshire Association (1911) and was for many years Secretary of the Dartmoor Preservation Association.

Right: Princess Mary, later to become our Queen, studies the card at the Huccaby Races of 1909. Her lifelong love of millinery confection is evident even at this early stage: she was a much-loved lady. Facing the Princess on the left of this picture is Robert Burnard, who shared her close and abiding interest in objects of beauty and antiquity.

Above: The rustic pavilion on the croquet lawn at Huccaby House which had done service as a Royal Box for the Huccaby Races of 1909. The small child perched on the cross-bar, her arm resting for support against her grandfather, Robert Burnard, was to become the wife of an English admiral. She is now Lady Sayer, the indomitable defender of Dartmoor, revered by conservationists and admired even by her opponents for her forthright and unceasing opposition to any proposal which threatens the quality of its landscape.

A family scene outside Huccaby House in 1894.

Well shod, warmly clad and intriguingly hatted (how did the ladies maintain their dignity, or head gear, in high winds?) this group of walkers, Robert Burnard among them, looks slightly tired after the hike.

Below: Jolly Lane Cottage, Hexworthy, 1889, home of Sally Satterley, a house which was said to have been built in one day by labourers while the landowners were revelling elsewhere: Sally's father lit a fire in the hearth before they returned and claimed this constituted a freehold!

Sally, 80 when this picture (*right*) was taken, was pursued by Baring-Gould who heard she was a singer of old folk-songs. But she would not sit down to sing: Baring-Gould had to follow her around her household tasks with a notebook, jotting down the ballads as Sally sang!

She was undaunted by raised eyebrows when she decided to work at nearby Eylesburrow tin mine. It was said that she could nail a shoe as well as any blacksmith, and could drive packhorses, cut peat or mow with a scythe as proficiently as any man. Not until 1901 did this indomitable character join her Maker.

The July of 1891 proved a most productive month for photographer Robert Burnard. There is an arrogant poise from the stiff-backed horsemen, in stark contrast to the hunched figure at the roadside: a group of Dartmoor gamins peep cautiously from the security of the cottage doorway. This is the hamlet of Ponsworthy.

Beatrice Chase, whose signature appears on this photograph of the Dun Stone, at Widecombe-in-the-Moor, wrote many romantic books about Dartmoor.

An eccentric, who was happy to adopt the title conferred upon her by an admirer, My Lady of the Moor, Beatrice claimed direct descent from the brother of Katherine Parr, last of King Henry VIII's wives.

Left: Largely, and somewhat surprisingly, tiny Ponsworthy is mostly ignored in the guide books. It occupies a sequestered position in a sheltered valley through which runs the West Webburn river. This old photograph, taken in the early years of this century, features the village street and the house owned by the shoemaker, Mr Warren.

Widecombe has done well from tourism throughout the century. The National Trust, having purchased the granite, fifteenth-century Church House (*left*), pictured to the right of the tree, has now opened it as a shop and information centre.

Below: Mr Kernick's wares, of pottery, postcards and Toby jugs, are grouped around two early Esso pumps: 'On view here', reads the sign, 'Guaranteed genuine, photos of the original Uncle Tom Cobley, his home, his chair and his will...'

Below left: The Old Inn, at Widecombe-in-the-Moor, in the 1920s, and there, still, to this day, little altered.

The present-day popularity of Widecombe Fair owes much to its musical association with the folk-song written down by Baring-Gould in the 1890s, and sung as a march by men of the Devonshire Regiment during the Boer War.

The tombstone in Spreyton churchyard (*above left*) marks the grave of Thomas Cobley, who died in 1844 aged 82 years, but this is not in memory of the original Tom Cobley. Uncle Tom himself died, at a great age, in the year 1794. His nephew inherited the estate, yet, sadly, seemed to have neglected to raise a memorial to his more famous uncle.

Uncle Tom's role at Widecombe Fair was played, in these old photographs, by Bert Dunn.

A jollier group of bounds-beaters it would be difficult to imagine than this one – all male – which posed on the clapper bridge near Widecombe in May, 1924.

The walking sticks are home manufactured, hazel, perhaps, and ash for a splash.

The custom of beating-the-bounds, though now a dying one, continues still, often through a septennial perambulation. Free fights, however, no longer mar these proceedings, as they often did before local government became so firmly established.

Some parishes were in the habit of moving a boundary stone (or two) into the confines of its neighbouring authority – needless to say, the correction was made at the earliest opportunity by those thus 'invaded' but the 'correction' was often over-generous!

With a cargo of 25 passengers, which included Mr and Mrs Bates, the village teachers, together with the Vicar of Widecombe, the Reverend E.C. Wood, the bespectacled, cigarette-smoking charabanc driver, would have been on his best behaviour.

Straw boaters for the middle-classes, and cloth cap for that elderly gentleman – was it the school janitor or the verger – sitting directly behind Mr Bates, and perfectly positioned to cuff the ear of any disorderly back-seat passenger.

This was 21 July 1920, the annual Widecombe School outing; the six-week summer holiday was looming large in the minds of these young pupils – and, doubtless, their teachers!

Postbridge and its clapper across the East Dart River. One of the
most interesting objects on Dartmoor, the clapper bridge is
almost 43 feet long, and much older than the village itself: it has
intrigued adults and delighted children for generations past.

Postbridge, 1893. On the cart, two unknown children. Standing, at the back, Lawrence Burnard (*centre*) and two friends. Seated (*left to right*), Dorothy Burnard (in front), her mother, Frances Louise Burnard, just behind her, and two unknown ladies. Standing, in front, with 'banjo' is the younger Charles Burnard. The Burnard family often stayed at the Greyhound, Postbridge, while Charles Burnard (senior) still 'reigned' at Huccaby House.

As functional as it was aesthetically harmonious this ancient
cottage at Higher Merripit, photographed by Burnard in August,
1892, looks as if it just grew out of the Moor. Note the preference
on Dartmoor for small windows, all the better to keep out the
rough weather.

The occupants of that snug, sheltered Dartmoor cottage at
Merripit were Mr and Mrs Cleave and their young daughter
who posed (*right*) beneath the porch for Mr Burnard. Note the
horse-shoe for luck and Mr Cleave's 'thatch' which perfectly
matches the well-worn roof of his home!

Left: Between 1883 and 1913 some 220 tons of black tin were extracted from the Golden Dagger Tin Mine, about half a mile south-east of the Warren House Inn on Dartmoor.

The site is one of the most interesting on the Moor, but great care must be taken in visiting it, as potentially, it is one of the most dangerous.

A great deal of money was invested after the mine sett was acquired, in 1880, by Moses Bawden, some £10,000; several new shafts were created, among them the Machine Shaft, which was sunk to a depth of more than 40 fathoms.

By 1920, when this photograph was taken, the heyday was over, but the mine was re-prospected again during the early years of the last war, when tin was in short supply, to assess the value of the spoil heaps. But all of interest that was found were the remains of an electro-magnetic separator – even that had been unsuccessful in separating the haematite from the black tin.

Such handsome vestiges of a bygone industry are rare indeed today. This machinery, already beyond repair, was photographed in the engine house of Owlacombe Mine, near Sigford, a terrain where granite gives way to shale. Owlacombe and its partner, Stormdown, were worked for tin in the seventeenth century, and became a profitable source of arsenic until the first world war.

With confident tread, Sabine Baring-Gould, steps out on a May morning in 1894. The camera is trained upon him, albeit a little shakily, by a devoted admirer, Robert Burnard.

They are together at Grimspound, the fantastic early Bronze Age village, whose hut circles had induced generations of earlier visitors to ascribe magical properties to the dull slabs of granite. The Reverend gentleman himself was no slouch when it came to adding a dash of fantasy to whet a jaded appetite.

It was Baring Gould and Burnard who supervised the excavation of these 24 huts, enclosed within a pound, in 1896. Their investigation was thorough and professional.

Baring-Gould, the squire-parson of Lewtrenchard, had an incurable love of the unusual in life. He scoured Europe to beautify his lovely home and its nearby church.

He wrote popular hymns such as, *Now The Day Is Over*, and the stirring *Onward Christian Soldiers* – and he was responsible for setting down for posterity some of the finest of English folk-songs.

Baring-Gould was devoted to the cause of protecting Dartmoor, and not surprisingly, was a founder member of the Dartmoor Preservation Association which, in 1983, celebrated its centenary. How that would have pleased him!

Long since submerged beneath the waters of the Fernworthy reservoir, this old clapper bridge, stoutly constructed, had survived the traffic of gentler times.

During the great drought of 1976, when Dartmoor was warmer even than the Mediterranean littoral, the reservoir waters receded and evaporated, revealing a vision of a lost landscape, of petrified tree stumps and ancient tracks.

No threat of inundation posed itself when this photograph was taken. Shortly after work upon the reservoir dam had begun, in the summer of 1938, a massive rainstorm struck Dartmoor.

It washed away a crane, and tons of mud had to be removed before work could continue.

Today, the area has become a honeypot where, no longer, silence broods over the historic enclosure of 'Fernworthie'. The conifer forest now reigns in consort with the ice-cream vans.

Assacombe row, now obliterated by canopies of conifers at
Fernworthy. Attributed to the 'Beaker' people, who decorated
their pottery ware with chevrons and elongated S patterns, the
avenue of stones was probably raised in early Bronze Age times.

Another of Dartmoor's stone rows, or avenues, this one as seen
early this century at Kes Tor.

Scorhill Stone Circle, undoubtedly one of the most impressive
remaining on Dartmoor and described by Samuel Rowe (1848)
as 'by far the finest example of the rude but venerable shrines of
Druidical worship in Devonshire'. Rowe was wrong about
Druidic involvement, but it may well have been the scene of
ceremonies, possibly sepulchral in nature, and reminiscent of
early Bronze Age ritual.

The primaeval splendour of such uncharted wilderness as that surrounding one of the several Wallabrook Bridges on Dartmoor (this stone footbridge crosses the 'Teign' Walla Brook) clearly intrigued the Victorian love of mysticism.

Then, as now, this is high moorland, a concentration of mystery and majesty where the imagination can run riot.

Few, if any of these clapper bridges are, however, earlier than medieval in construction, but this Walla Brook Bridge has provided safe passage for shepherd, sheep and ramblers for centuries past. Not, as some early Victorian writers would have us believe, for the movements of Druids, celebrating ancient rites.

In the background (*left*) rises Watern Tor, the domed hill that forms the eastern limit of Dartmoor's great central basin and of the Forest of Dartmoor itself.

Note the luxuriant growth of heather of 100 years ago.

To the Victorian, who captioned this photograph, this was Castor – today, it is known as Kes Tor. Its vast mass, with its many rock basins, commands wide views especially over the Teign basin.

An old Devon saying insists that, where rushes grow, horses can go. And as if to prove it, not only horses but a cart also found themselves in the eye of Robert Burnard's camera near Cranmere Pool on 6 August 1892. The Pool, of course, is not a pool at all – but that's another story!

Richard Perrott was one of the four sons of James Perrott, the Dartmoor guide who, in 1854, set up the first Dartmoor 'Postbox' at Cranmere Pool.

The most celebrated of modern Dartmoor authors, Mr Eric Hemery, refers in his book, *High Dartmoor*, to a *Times* article of 1934.

Perrott, then 95, received a letter of thanks from the Duchess of Kent for his wedding gift of trout and salmon flies. Her Royal Highness expressed her amazement that Richard was able to perform such fine work without the aid of glasses.

And, the *Times* article added, Mr Perrott had, in the past, made flies for such notabilities as Charles Dickens, Charles Kingsley, John Morley, Baring-Gould and the author of *Lorna Doone*.

Belstone Tor, and the Irishman's Wall.

The village of Belstone, which lies at the northern tip of the ring
of commons which circle the central Forest of Dartmoor like a
necklace of pearls.

The Old Rectory of Belstone village (*above right*): of such scenes,
Eden Phillpotts wrote (in *The Secret Women*): 'Belstone village
appeared in a snug and clustered congeries of little dwellings
that faced all ways and exhibited every beauty of whitewash
and rosy-wash, old thatch and venerable slate.'

Mid-June, 1923, and the community of Belstone 'Beat the
Bounds'. The ceremony is an ancient one, with proprietorial and
ecclesiastical associations, since it was originally concerned not
only with parish boundaries but also the blessing of crops.
Belstone was said to beat its bounds once every seven years,
and habitually moved one of the boundary stones a little way
into South Tawton Parish! The matter was invariably redressed,
however, since South Tawton dutifully moved the stone back
when it beat its own bounds!
Such delightful traditions on Dartmoor have been
undermined, in more recent years, by a dreary succession of
unwanted local government reforms.

A romantic view of Okehampton Castle, erected around 1300 for
residential as much as defensive purposes. The castle, owned by
the Department of Environment, is no longer in such a ruinous
or overgrown state.

Meldon Viaduct, a notable example of railway engineering,
carrying the line 160 feet over a deep ravine.

'I didn't know you was on this,' wrote the sender of this postcard seventy years ago. 'Leslie saw it first.' The surprised Mrs Finch who bought this card of Okehampton Market did so, undoubtedly, because she spotted her husband, Tom, in the picture! Tom, thumbs in waistcoat, and wearing his bowler at a rakish angle, is at bottom right.

Within the space of eleven days in 1910, Okehampton witnessed two military funerals, those of Gunner William Devine (*above*) of the 122nd Battery of the Royal Field Artillery and Sergeant William Whittaker (*above right*) of the 119th Battery RFA.

Young Devine, a twenty-year-old Liverpool man, died on his first day's training at the Okehampton Battle Camp, crushed to death beneath the wheels of a gun wagon which overturned when it struck a boulder at the roadside.

It was, reported *The Western Morning News* at the time, 'an untimely end to a promising young soldier'. Devine was buried on the hillside churchyard with full military honours. The gun carriage which bore his body from the camp to the churchyard was an eighteen-pounder from the battery.

Sergeant Whittaker died 'with tragic suddenness on his way to Devonport Military Hospital'.

The bearers were eight sergeant-comrades and, behind the coffin which was borne on a gun carriage, the deceased's charger was led, followed by six trumpeters.

The Band of the local company of volunteers followed the firing party and played 'The Dead March in Saul'. The service, said the newspaper report, was conducted with the impressive rites of the Roman Catholic Church.

The streets of Okehampton were lined with spectators for both funerals: the Army, which had won the licences to train on the Moor in the previous century, was welcome in the town (*below* 1909), as it is to this day.

Left: Be-ribboned in splendour, this was Rifleman Ward, a native of tiny Exbourne, whose exploits with the rifle made him as popular, in his time, as any superstar of the present era.

Ward achieved the then near-impossible by winning the Queen's Prize at Bisley twice – in 1897 and 1900. Only one other man had ever matched such marksmanship before.

At Exeter and Okehampton, the Devon Rifleman, who had brought glory to his county, was accorded civic receptions: the Shire celebrated their hero of the hour.

Rifleman Ward's private life was marred by tragedy: his wife died from terrible burns when the turpentine and beeswax she was mixing together ignited.

He – a gentle and retiring man, and a modest one, despite this show of medals – died in 1917 at the comparatively early age of fifty.

This photograph is a rarity, and was taken by the Dartmoor photographers Lugg and Son. Today, Ward's achievement is largely forgotten except in the sporting halls of fame.

The River Taw, flowing northwards like a silver ribbon, towards its rendezvous with the sea near Barnstaple.

Long before the tyranny of trunk roads and juggernauts,
Sticklepath basks peacefully in the warmth of the noon-day sun.
Finch's Foundry harnessed water power to create tools, becoming
a saw mill and foundry combined. The foundry turned out no
fewer than thirty types of agricultural tools – everything from
implements for cutting peat to scoops for the china-clay industry.
Even housewives called in to have their smoothing irons
'smoothed' on the emery wheel. Once a stronghold of Quakers,
it attracted the attention – and preaching – of John Wesley:
interestingly enough, Uncle Tom Cobley's fellow horsemen
were all said to have come from Sticklepath, the second cottage
on the right was said to be Bill Brewer's.

Wearing waistcoats and cloth caps as the uniform of their era, these Finch Foundry workers at Sticklepath were the craftsmen whose workmanship was renowned within and beyond the boundaries of Dartmoor.

They were: *Back row* (*standing*) W. Westaway (South Zeal), Jack Powesland and Christy Osborne. *Centre* (*standing*) John Mallett, A.G. Finch, Joe Hellier and Aubrey Tucker. *Front row* (*seated*) Alf Hooper, Laurence Taylor, Mr Gee (*astride the wheel*).

Tunes of glory from trumpet and tuba, drum and harmonium
resounded across Dartmoor from the Sticklepath Village Band.

In this old photograph, taken around 1890 outside the sloping
grounds of the Sticklepath Board School, the band accompanied
the children of the village Sunday School on their anniversary day.

Right: Olditch Farmhouse, near Sticklepath, a photograph taken
when farmer R. Cole's cart (dated 1889) was still comparatively
new. Part of the house, on the steep road from Sticklepath to
Exeter, exists to this day.

There's a whisper down the field where the year has shot her yield and the ricks stand gray in the sun, singing:– 'Over then, come over, for the bee has quit the clover and your Dartmoor summer's done.'
With apologies to Kipling – stacking hay at Sticklepath, 1890.

Ramsley Copper Mine, South Zeal, where a 50-foot pumping wheel raised water to work a 33-foot wheel for crushing ore. The mine itself, surrounded by its waste tips, appears to have burrowed itself out into the landscape like a vast molehill.

South Zeal was known once as Irishman's Town, thanks to the presence of Irish labourers in the mines nearby. But the Oxenham Arms (*below*) has nothing to do with Erin, though the legend associated with the name is as fantastic as any tale which emerged from the land of leprechauns. With the Oxenhams is connected the tradition of the White Bird, said to appear as a forewarning of the death of the head of the family. Readers of Charles Kingsley's *Westward Ho!* will be familiar with the legend.

Susannah Finch, the poetess who wrote that marriage is like a
Devonshire lane (full of unexpected events!) stands in the door
of her general grocery and tailor's shop at South Tawton. On the
right is her son, William Albert, the tailor, often to be found
sitting cross-legged in his workshop, like all tailors of old.

Upper: The obelisk pinnacles of the big granite church of St Andrew rise beguilingly through the trees near the village smithy at South Tawton.

Lower: The Cross Tree, South Tawton, a venerable elm in a village noted for its interesting dwellings: 'Thought this would make a change from Xmas cards' wrote the sender of this postcard, at the beginning of this century. The elm, like the writer, has succumbed, to the march of time.

Demure and unmistakably Devonian, this cottage, full of
summery charm, smothered richly in roses, stands in
Throwleigh. It is 1890. New-fangled wider windows are
beginning to replace the fenestration of small panes, and the
handsome semi-circular arched granite entrance door is partly
hidden by the over-slated porch. Wire netting? To protect the
flower beds from the roaming ravenous wild ponies.

Gidleigh, circa 1893. *Left to right*, on the brake, Charles Burnard (junior) and an unknown boy. Seated, Dorothy Burnard (Robert Burnard's younger daughter) and, standing, arms linked, Lawrence Burnard and his mother, Frances Louise Burnard (Robert Burnard's wife).

Left: A fifteenth-century church, a restaurant, the remains of a late Norman castle and a few houses, combine to make up the Dartmoor village of Gidleigh. 'Little Silver (Gidleigh) is a hamlet of almost beggarly simplicity,' wrote novelist Eden Phillpotts of this place.

Forlorn and sadly neglected as it appeared in this Victorian photograph, Gidleigh, whose history is closely interwoven with that of Chagford, is situated in a particularly lovely area. Only part of the small keep of the castle survives, in detail similar to Okehampton Castle.

Some say that much earlier, this was the birthplace of Queen Gydda, mother of King Harold, who died at Hastings in 1066, and of Edith, who became the wife of Edward The Confessor.

Risdon wrote in his *Survey*: 'As you coast the cliffs from Dawlish, you have in view the outlet of the River Teign, so called by the Britons, for that it is straightly pent with narrow banks, whose fountain is to be fetched from the forest of Dartmoor, near the Gidley Hills, where the ancient progeny of the Prouzes had their castle, whereof most were called William.'

In 1900, the Reverend Sabine Baring-Gould, parson, poet and hymn-writer lauded Chagford for its 'salubrious climate, incomparable scenery, ready hospitality, rural sweetness and archaeological interest'.

'Whither the writers pointed with their pens,' he wrote, 'thither the public ran, and Chagford was made. It has now every appliance suitable – pure water, electric lighting, a bicycle shop, and doctors to patch broken heads and set broken limbs of those upset from their bikes.'

Timeless though the market square now appears, the quaint market house, nick-named the 'Pepper Pot', was built in 1862, replacing 'The Shambles' – the old slaughter house – which stood on the site.

Chagford Square also once boasted a Stannary Court building, which is said to have collapsed, suddenly, in 1617, after a witness swore, on oath, that if he was lying, he hoped the building would fall upon him! It did!

The town was one of Devon's four Stannary, or tin, centres, where the metal was taken by the miners to be weighed, assessed, taxed and stamped. Tin brought Chagford wealth, especially between the twelfth and fifteenth centuries: the activities of the tinners are to be seen to this day all over surrounding Dartmoor and, as late as 1904, the lodes were still being worked for the precious metal.

This Victorian photograph, of Mill Street, Chagford, depicted
the house built, probably, around 1820, by a Mr Berry, who had
earlier opened a blanket and serge mill near Chagford Bridge.

Window tax was not repealed until the 1850s, but doubtless
the owners found it no inconvenience to put up with darkened
rooms – it saved the cost of fashionable Victorian window
drapes!

The three 'ancients' who formed a triangle of gossip in the
street, clearly had nothing to fear from the motor vehicle, which
was not to make its entry in Chagford until around 1917.

Mr Berry's handsome house has now become the Moorlands
Hotel.

According to the Domesday Book of 1086, 'Chagford was held by Dodo in the time of King Edward.' Our knowledge of Dodo has become obscured in the mists of time, but Rushford Mill (*right*) and Rushford Tower (*below*), from where these views of early Chagford were obtained, are upon a site where Roman coins were found, though how they came to be there is unknown.

Chagford, a Saxon word meaning Gorse Ford – where the River Teign was forded – grew from a manorial farm into a hamlet, and then into a village in a relatively short time.

It quickly became a focus, complete with a church and market. Over the long line of stepping stones the Rushford millers would have borne their sacks of grain, to be ground exceeding small.

The Strand, Chagford, when postcards cost a half-penny to post.

The village blacksmith, Chagford –

Far from the madding crowd's ignoble strife
Their sober wishes never learn'd to stray;
Along the cool, sequester'd vale of life
They kept the noiseless tenor of their way.

From heights where snow and ice cling longer together than anywhere else in southern England, the waters of the North Teign rush down off Dartmoor. The South Teign joins in the tumble of the rivers at Leigh Bridge, Chagford.

Much more than the sylvan beauty of this meeting place was apparent, however, to the eyes of Dr John Archibald Purves of Taunton who, in 1919, formed a plan to harness the power of the water for electricity generation by means of eight reservoirs.

But Purves's schemes, which might have spelt the end to such sanctuaries as Leigh Bridge, came to naught. The House of Lords rejected both Bills in 1937.

Nothing daunted, the North Devon Water Board picked up some of the pieces in 1956 with its Taw Marsh reservoir scheme.

Only at Mary Tavy on Dartmoor did any hydro-electric scheme come to fruition: interestingly, it is now the last place (together with the Morwellham hydro-electric station) where the Central Electricity Generating Board generates electricity in Devon and Cornwall.

The handsome cross on Week Down, near Chagford, with its incised Maltese Crosses cut into each face, was moved in the 1860s to prevent it from falling down. Many of Dartmoor's stone crosses are still to be found in old walls or acting as gate posts: hill farmers found a practical use for them!

All cob wants is a good hat and a good pair of shoes, states an old Devon saying. A solid roof and a sound plinth are the golden rules if the cob houses – of unbaked earth construction – are to be kept dry.

Just as cob was a natural material for this Chagford cottage (*left*), so thatch, with generous eaves – was an automatic choice for a roof.

Chagford's Three Crowns Hotel, however, is made of sterner stuff, which is as well (*below*).

For two tragedies are associated with it in days gone by.

The pious Mary Whyddon was, so tradition would have it, shot by a jealous lover at the entrance to this ancient inn when returning from her wedding in the year 1641.

And two years later, Sidney Godolphin, royalist and poet, 'A young gentleman of incomparable parts' according to the historians of the day, was shot by a musket in the porch of the Three Crowns.

Precious Sidney, whose Cornish relatives were to rise to almost supreme power during the reign of Queen Anne, was said to be so refined a creature that 'a little rayne or winde would disorder him'. The gentle creature is said still to haunt Chagford, a victim of the Civil War.

Both the cob cottage, known locally as Bishop's Cottage, and the Inn, continue to survive, as they have done so sturdily down the long centuries.

Chagford never experienced the glamour of the railway. Had
the line originally proposed been built, however, through the
Teign Gorge from Dunsford, it would have been one of the
loveliest in Britain. Beeching, of course, would have closed it –
so perhaps nothing was lost!

Instead, visitors relied upon the 'stage' coach or, a little later,
the Omnibus link.

Both examples of horsepower are seen in these photographs
about to draw away from Chagford's Globe Inn, the original
post-house, to their Exeter railway station destination.

Below right: Early delivery vans in Chagford.

Of all the town's glories, Chagford Church remains now, as it did in this photograph taken at the turn of this century, the crown.

Long before its dedication in 1261 by the Bishop of Exeter, a church stood here.

Priests were not only expected to fight for their King, it appears, they also dabbled in commercial interests. Part ownership of some of the nearby tin mines enabled a little of that wealth to be invested to the greater glory of God.

Dedicated to St Michael, Chagford Church, its handsome tower completed in the fifteenth century, forms the heart about which the town was built.

A hundred years ago it still lacked its processional cross of aluminium, made from a wrecked Zeppelin, but it certainly then contained the remarkable monument to Sir John Wyddon (1575) of the early Renaissance period.

The Spinsters' Rock cromlech, near Chagford, collapsed in a heap in January, 1862, and it is to the antiquarian, G. Waring Ormerod that we owe its resurrection.

It was Ormerod who wrote, in 1876, some years before this photograph was taken, of old Chagford: 'Those who remember the quaint old town with its many thatched roofs and casement windows may possibly look with regret upon the alterations which have been made, but they are only parts of a series of changes that are everywhere taking place.'

The cromlech, or dolmen, is the finest of its kind on Dartmoor, and this stone table on a tripod of stones marks, simply, a place of sepulture.

According to legend, it was raised by three spinsters, all 'yarn spinners', who diverted themselves by building the dolmen!

From Dolmen we move to Tolmen, an object clearly of irresistible interest to the Victorian photographer from Chagford who may have been aware then, as now, that a journey through the hole in the centre of the stone was reckoned to be a cure for rheumatism.

Unfortunately, those suffering from such an ill, might do themselves further mischief from the exercise!

The scoutmaster in this 1911 photograph (*right*) was Harry Price, one of the most remarkable Dartmoor men of this century.

Harry came out of the Royal Navy with the rank of Petty Officer in 1907, having travelled the world. As a young sailor, he was stationed at Devonport, and his chief joy was to walk across the Moor, diagonally, from that world-famous dockyard to Chagford.

Young Price was a man of many parts, with a rare gift for painting and as an angler. He had run away to sea from Birmingham, where he had been born in 1877.

It was during an excursion across Dartmoor that the young matelot strayed into a Shangri-la – at Fingle Bridge (*below*).

Harry was so deeply moved by the beauty and quiet of this lovely green gorge that he wept with joy, and even the church bells seemed to beckon him to Drewsteignton. He resolved to make it his home.

And home it became, for him, but not before he sailed around the world aboard HMS *Ophir* which carried the Duke and Duchess of York – later to become King George V and Queen Mary – to all parts of the British Empire on their 1901 Royal Tour. His superbly written and illustrated account of that voyage became, in 1980, a best-seller when Webb and Bower published it as a follow-up to the famous *Diary of an Edwardian Lady*.

Harry returned, as he had promised he would, to Drewsteignton, and lived an almost idyllic existence in and around the valley he so loved from 1907 until he was recalled to naval duties in 1915.

His scout troop in this old photograph were all boys of Upcott House School, Okehampton, a private establishment for young gentlemen, most of whom, as officers, laid down their lives in the terrible conflict between 1914 and 1918.

But for a short span, at least, Harry Price and his young charges enjoyed the blissful countryside near Fingle Bridge, where he taught them the variety of countryside skills which were second nature to him.

Drewsteignton (*above 1889 and right circa 1910*), a scene that has altered little for all the passage of time. The all-granite church of Holy Trinity rises high and handsomely above the village centre.

When, in the mid-nineteenth century, antiquarians believed Dartmoor to have been the haunt of Druids, it was concluded that Drewsteignton meant The Druid's Town on the Teign. At the time of the Domesday Book it was called Teintona.

Right: A Harry Price photograph of a Harry Price snowman! The small boy with the moon-like features standing front right is Parker Walker, son of Edwin Lutyens's clerk of works. At that time, March 1914, Castle Drogo was still under construction.

Above: At a cottage door in Drewsteignton in her long white apron, stands Jessie Ashplant, mother-in-law of Harry Price. It was she who founded the tea house at Fingle Bridge, now renowned as the Angler's Rest, and owned by her grandson, Jack Price, to this day.

Left: For ten years, from 1897 until 1907, Jessie Ashplant of Drewsteignton made and sold pots of tea in the open air near Fingle Bridge. In 1907, the first tea shelter was built. Its roof, of corrugated iron, was criticised by the local landowner as unsightly. Jessie covered it with furze and bracken.

The shelter survived, until 1929, when it was replaced: that lasted until 1957, when the Angler's Arms was built on the site. Jessie, her daughter Ethel, and Ethel's son, Jack Price, have been tending to the needs of visitors to Fingle Bridge for almost 90 years.

Two great Dartmoor characters, forever playing practical jokes on each other, were Alfred Mudge (*left*), landlord of the Drewe Arms, and Bill Williams, a 'traveller' in farm medicines.

Alfred, or 'Boss' as he was known, was the eldest son in a family noted for its longevity (one generation alone kept the Drewe Arms for nigh on 100 years) and the fact that at least one ancestor had sat in the tin 'Parliament' on Crockern Tor.

Billy, or 'Johnny Fortnight' as he was called, since it was his habit to call once every two weeks, and 'Boss' were firm friends, ever ready for fun and games!

It was Harry Price who snapped them together.

Right: 'Boss' – Alfred Mudge – and 'Missus' – his wife – outside the pub originally known as the Druid's Arms, but renamed the Drewe Arms with the persuasion of the powerful new neighbouring landowner, Julius Drewe. It was Drewe, who made a fortune in selling groceries through his chain of shops, Home and Colonial Stores, who commissioned the great English architect, Edwin Lutyens, to build for him Castle Drogo, a medieval-style castle on a magnificent outcrop of granite overlooking the Teign Gorge. Castle Drogo, completed in 1931, is now owned by The National Trust.

A photograph taken by Harry Price prior to the function at the Long Room in the Drewe Arms at which presided Captain Morrison Bell, MP for the Mid-Devon constituency.

Morrison-Bell was an extremely popular Tory, whose picture hangs over the fireplace in this photograph. Elections at that time were fiercely-contested and often rowdy affairs.

'Stick to Bell for Mid-Devon' were the rousing words of one of the campaigning songs of the era.

Below: For all the world like a set from *My Fair Lady*, this 1910 scene was recorded at Drewsteignton. The photograph was taken by Chapman, a well-known Dawlish cameraman. The two ladies being escorted in this picture are not brides, as may at first be thought, but bridesmaids.

It is known that the bride's brother, a Mr Edgar Pillar, was a mathematical genius who worked with Marconi. Edgar, however, was not given to temperance habit!

He had set out to walk to the wedding from Exeter Station but got as far as Tedburn St Mary where the refreshments offered at the Kings' Arms were over-liberally imbibed. Edgar never arrived to see his sister's wedding, and had to be content, like us, with a photograph of the scene.

The handsome car on the left is the first to be owned by anyone in Drewsteignton, a wonder in its day.

Left: Drewsteignton, 3 July 1915. A bride – but no groom!

The reason was remarkable, but really quite simple, for the groom was none other than Harry Price, and he was the only man in the village who owned a camera!

The bride was Ethel Ashplant, and the picture was taken outside her mother's cottage.

Right: The Rector of Drewsteignton, Richard Peek, neath Fingle Bridge. Peek, related to the owners of Peek Freane, the well known biscuit manufacturers, advised Mrs Jessie Ashplant (Harry Price's mother-in-law to-be) to set up a tea shop at Fingle Bridge after the Old Mill burnt down in a fire in July, 1894. The Mill was never rebuilt.

The reverend gentleman seems to have preferred sea trout to Matins, and he especially enjoyed a cup of tea during his fishing expeditions. The Old Mill owners having departed after the fire, Peek set about to repair the deficiency in his day's enjoyment – hence his advice to Jessie!

Below: Lifelong Dartmoor forester, Oliver Giles Gidleigh, taking lunch in his roughly-hewn shelter in a plantation near Drewsteignton. One of the village's three bootmakers would have fashioned those stout boots, and the blacksmith would have shod them. Dartmoor men invariably wore hob-nailed boots, even for Sunday best, and, it is said, they would perform step dances in that footgear on fourteen-inch platforms of wood placed in the rear of farm wagons. For all their weight, the boots carried them as light as a feather.

Oliver Giles's father was the last cooper to work in Drewsteignton in the days when village communities had to be self-sufficient to survive.

The Cross Tree, Moretonhampstead, 1908.

Left: Among the many splendid marksmen born on Dartmoor, Percy Stanbury was one of the greatest.

Percy's father was a farmer, and the boy led a lonely, isolated existence outside little Drewsteignton. His father bought him an airgun, and young Percy became proficient at shooting wasps when they were in flight!

When he moved to a 12-bore gun, and clay pigeons, it came to him like child's play.

He grew up to become a champion of champions, and represented England no fewer than 26 times. In later life, he coached both the Duke of Edinburgh and Prince Charles.

Percy still reckons that his greatest feat was performed in the Fingle Bridge valley when, armed with a repeater 12-bore, he had five dead pigeons in the air – all at the same time! He repeated the remarkable demonstration of his skill for the benefit of the TV cameras.

Crack shot though he was, however, Percy, who is now 90 years of age, invariably states that his first love was sea trout fishing with the late Harry Price (who died in 1965 aged 88 years) at Fingle Bridge.

Below left: Little excuse was needed to make merry at Moretonhampstead, and the town which celebrated the coronations of the Royal Georges in the eighteenth and nineteenth centuries with grand balls and fetes, joyously acknowledged the succession of King George V in the twentieth.

Left: Moretonhampstead en fete once again – this time in celebration of a royal visitor.

Below: Market Day at Moretonhampstead around the turn of the century. A place of gas lamps, and Police sergeants to whom road traffic problems were largely unknown: from the presence of food on one of the pavement counters health regulations were unheard of. The cheerful aproned shop assistant near the policeman holds a pole with a hook, ready to pull down the shop sun blinds.

Right: The village cross on the edge of the green at North Bovey. For a time, William Crossing related, it served the purpose of a footbridge, but was set up in its present situation in 1829 by the Reverend J.P. Jones, then parish curate.

Below: The Ring O' Bells, North Bovey, a hostelry popular with Dartmoor hill farmers not least because of its stables where many steeple-chasers have been bred over the years.

NORTH BOVEY

Bowerman's Nose – a Dartmoor rock idol some 25 feet tall, its
fantastic formation created by the whim of all the weathers.

Below: Dartmoor is rough country for the hunting man – and the fox!

Some remarkable characters have emerged, not least Sir Walter Carew, who founded the South Devon in 1830. Wealthy, arrogant, he rode as he drank, almost without ceasing. It's said he once told the Lord Lieutenant's lady: 'Time is wasted on women which you can give to the hounds!'

This Hunt Meet was photographed at Manaton outside one of the village's Domesday manors.

Right: Dartmoor has been a fruitful seed plot for many artists and writers, not least John Galsworthy, who lived at a farm between Manaton and North Bovey. Bernard Shaw visited him there.

When he was not writing – his output was prodigious, and the Manaton Edition of his work contains 30 volumes – Galsworthy loved to ride across the Moor on horseback.

He became well known locally for his generosity, and nationally, of course, for *The Forsyte Saga.* He died, in London, in 1933.

St Winifred's Church at Manaton, a village off the beaten track, but none the worse for that. John Galsworthy lived not far distant.

Below left: Roses wind a romantic course over whitewashed cottage walls in Lustleigh. The Primrose Cafe is now to be found where the thatched forge once stood.

The railway had reached Lustleigh, and those who feared for the changes it might make were proved only partly correct. Lustleigh time was railway time; minutes hadn't mattered much previously, only the way in which they were spent.

Those who wish to explore the further charm of this village may do so through Cecil Torr's *Small Talk at Wreyland* – a classic which owes its origins to Wreyland, Lustleigh.

Below: Round the Maypole trit, trit, trot – See what a Maypole we have got – Fine and gay, trip away, happy is our new May Day.

Garlands galore decorate little Miss Olive Chudley, who was May Queen at Lustleigh in 1906.

104

Left: The caption to this post-war photograph (probably taken around 1920) reads, simply: 'Bovey Tracey Outing'.

Their names may be forgotten, but the place where they made this stop is unmistakable.

Behind the cameraman is Bedford Square, and at the back of the group rises the Tavistock Town Hall built by the 7th Duke of Bedford from the profits from an industry in which the forefathers of some of these gentlemen might well have been engaged – mining.

Below left: Carnival time in Bovey Tracey circa 1912. 'Nigger' minstrels, elephant, Domino and the upside-down man, said to have been a Mr Bowden.

Below: Dartmoor was never especially noted for its music-making, though there were folk-singers and versatile exponents of the broom-dance, an art form which seems to have disappeared.

Brass bands were, however, in great demand, at concerts in parish halls, in fair grounds, meadows and at carnival time.

If this Haytor 5th Company Volunteer battalion of the Devon Regiment played half as well as they looked, then their music must have been a memorably sweet experience indeed. The photograph, from the Dartington Archives, was taken in the early 1900s.

Romany ways and Romany days upon Dartmoor. Robert Burnard found these gipsies on Spitchwick Common, presumably a favourite site in the first decade of this century for these 'travellers'.

The caravanserai of modern-day tinkers, with their mobile homes, now centres much closer to the fringes of urban sprawl.

In the old days, on Dartmoor, their presence did not give as much offence, perhaps, and the superstitious in Society would have hesitated to turn away a gipsy from the doorstep without a purchase of some trinket or a bundle of clothes pegs. Romany curses were to be avoided!

It is a small and very cold-looking group which huddles about this camp fire. And what concoction, one wonders, did that cast-iron frying pan contain?

Above: Hay, or to be correct, Heytor, with its immense granite bulk, has been enormously popular with visitors to Dartmoor: it was the scene, in the late 1960s of a 'love-in', a concept totally alien to the climate of opinion at the time this photograph was taken.

Below: 'And far away, beyond the last peaks and saliences southward, stretched a horizon of dazzling and colourless light, where sea-girdled earth and Devon rolled dark against the liquid brilliance of the Channel lifted beyond it.' Eden Phillpotts – *Orphan Dinah* (1920).

The Vulcan of Holne, 1892.

Holne Vicarage, birthplace of Charles Kingsley, the Geminian who gave the world such literary treasures as *Westward Ho!* (written at Bideford), a book saturated with scenes from Devon. Kingsley was born in 1819 at a time when his father was temporary curate-in-charge at Holne: the vicarage was rebuilt in 1832, some 60 years before this photograph was taken.

Oh England is a pleasant place for them that's rich and high,
But England is a cruel place for such poor folks as I.

Above: If the battle of Waterloo was won on the playing fields of Eton, what, we may ask, did these eurhythmics on the playing fields of Buckfastleigh achieve?

The photograph is undated, but the fashionable cloche hats of the 1920s are in evidence among spectators.

Nearby (but out of sight) at that time, the Benedictine community of Buckfast Abbey (consecrated in 1932) were still toiling at their monumental task.

Left: Buckfast Abbey, was rebuilt early this century on the foundations of the old, created first around 1018. Its reconstruction makes an outstanding story of tenacity and faith. One monk, Brother Peter, trained a small group of brothers to assist him, and rebuilt this magnificent edifice in 31 years. For centuries earlier, a route (The Jobbers Path) ran between Buckfast and Tavistock Abbeys.

Persistent is the legend that would have us believe that here, Childe the Hunter, was caught in a snow storm, and endeavouring to save himself, cut open the belly of his horse and crawled inside the beast for shelter. Childe was said to have perished, his lands falling into the hands of the Abbots of Tavistock. When, in the 1970s it was proposed to construct a vast reservoir at this lonely site (Swincombe), promises were made that the tomb would be removed to the reservoir water's edge with the same reverence afforded to the Egyptian antiquities at Abu Simbel! The reservoir was never built.

Stands the clock at ten to three? And is there honey still for tea?

The Church of St Peter, at Meavy, dates, in part at least, from Norman times, and if Loudon's Arboretum is correct, then the Meavy oak – a battered specimen even around 1900 when this photograph was taken – has stood on guard at the lichgate since at least then.

Timid entreaties have been made to have it removed – the topmost branches are a threat to double-decker buses – the villagers, however, will hear nothing of such sacrilege.

Beneath its boughs can be seen a cross, the shaft of which was discovered by a former rector, the Reverend W.A.G. Gray, who was responsible for setting it back once more on its old pedestal.

To the left, the narrow road winds around towards Yelverton, between tall Devon hedgebanks carpeted creamy yellow in springtime with primroses.

So little has changed in the past 80 or more years since Robert Burnard captured this group of curious spectators on Meavy Green.

The Royal Oak Inn, now owned by the parish council, produces a revenue for its ratepayers.

The village green is now an expanse of grass, in contrast to the bare and stony plot of yesteryear.

The Royal Oak, gnarled and mis-shapen, is far from finished however, and seems set to see in yet another century or more.

The road to Yelverton (or Elford Town, as many may still have referred to it up to 1914) was hardly paved with gold.

But the town was, then, on the point of becoming a favourite residential area for those who worked in Plymouth and who owned a car.

A pile of stone on the right in this photograph awaits the attention, doubtless, of the builders.

Roborough Down had yet to be fenced, to keep cars and wild ponies apart.

Harrowbeer airfield, constructed during the last War, lies in the future, when it would occupy the spacious area to the left of this picture.

Almost impossible to believe, too, that this is now the most heavily-used of visitor and commuter highways on the Moor, and that gentle, undulating slope is now a motorist's speed track.

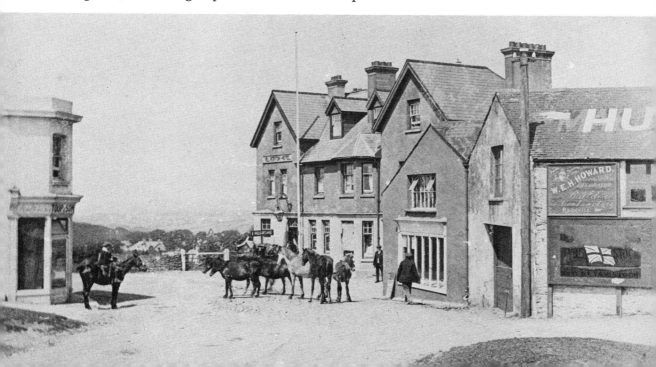

A scene from Victorian England, and note, please, the ladies'
gloves – de rigueur for the rambler of the time.

Left: The 'knowing' physicians had, for many years, sent their
convalescent patients to enjoy the benefits of the balmy, bracing
breezes of the gorse and heather-clad downs around Yelverton.

Rounded up, from Roborough Down nearby, these healthy
looking Dartmoor ponies await the next move – and that would
not, in 1910, have been to a knacker's yard or to the 'delights' of
a Channel crossing.

The nation needed those animals then.

The Yelverton Hotel occupies the centre of this old photograph,
the shopkeepers' names – Toop and Howard – are to be found
to this day in the district, and still in business, though no longer
in these premises in the area known now as Leg O' Mutton Corner.

Dartmoor Guides may come and go, but the name of William Crossing will live on.

Born in Plymouth in 1847, Crossing devoted a lifetime to the study of the Moor: his *Guide to Dartmoor* was published at three shillings, complete, by *The Western Morning News*, in 1909.

It is now justly described as a classic.

He made little profit from it, or from other works which flowed from his pen.

Eden Phillpotts, the descriptive writer, provided an introduction to Crossing's *Dartmoor Cot* stories.

'To say that no man knows Dartmoor so well as Crossing is to utter a truism. Her present and her past are familiar to him; her mountains and rivers are his friends; he has lived many years of his own life upon her bosom; and the very many sad and beautiful, stern and strange stories from her prehistoric and mediaeval past are his.'

Impecunious, and something of a recluse at the end of his life, William Crossing died in a Plymouth nursing home in September, 1928, and was buried at Mary Tavy on the Moor he so loved and understood.

'The poet, the local historian, the archaeologist and the writer who turns his gaze towards the realms of fancy have found work for their hands to do on Dartmoor,' he wrote, 'and shall continue to be its Chroniclers, that those who love it shall read something of its story.'

ACKNOWLEDGMENTS

The author and publisher wish to thank, in particular, Eric Hemery for his permission to use two extracts from *High Dartmoor* (Robert Hale, 1983) and, for their unfailing kindness and assistance with information and photographs the following: Vice-Admiral Sir Guy and Lady Sayer, Michael and Hilary Wreford (Okehampton), Bob Barron and Margery Pyne (Sticklepath), Jack Price and his family at Fingle Bridge, Percy Middleweek (Widecombe), the Dartington Archives, Plymouth Local History Library and the various people who have loaned photographs. We are also indebted to Tom Salmon for suggested sources of photographs.

Also Available

EXMOOR IN THE OLD DAYS

by Rosemary Anne Lauder. 147 old photographs. The author perceptively shows that Exmoor is not only the most beautiful of our Westcountry moors but is also rich in history and character: a world of its own in fact. '...*contains scores of old photographs and picture postcards...will provide a passport for many trips down memory lane...*'

Bideford Gazette

STRANGE STORIES FROM DEVON

by Rosemary Anne Lauder and Michael Williams. 46 photographs.
Strange shapes and places—strange characters— the man they couldn't hang, and a Salcombe mystery, the Lynmouth disaster and a mysterious house are only some of the strange stories.
'*A riveting read*'   The Plymouth Times
'...*well-written and carefully edited*'
Monica Wyatt, Teignmouth Post & Gazette

VIEWS OF OLD DEVON

Rosemary Anne Lauder provides the text for more than 200 old postcards, evocative of a world and a way of life that has gone. Words and pictures combine to produce a book that will delight all who love Devon.
'*Only the camera can turn back the clock like this.*'
The Sunday Independent

AROUND GLORIOUS DEVON

by David Young. 148 photographs.
David Young, well known in the Westcountry as TSW's roving architect, takes us on a personally-conducted tour of his glorious Devon.
'...*proves as good a guide in print as he is on the small screen.*'

Judy Diss, Herald Express

LEGENDS OF DEVON

by Sally Jones. 60 photographs and drawings. Devon is a mine of folklore and myth. Here in a journey through legendary Devon, Sally Jones brings into focus some fascinating tales, showing us that the line dividing fact and legend is an intriguing one.
'...*Sally Jones has trodden the path of legendary Devon well...*'

Tavistock Times

DARTMOOR PRISON
by Rufus Endle. 35 photographs.
A vivid portrait of the famous prison on the moor stretching from 1808—with rare photographs taken inside today.
'The bleak Devon cage's 170 year history...fascinatingly sketched by one of the Westcountry's best known journalists Rufus Endle...the man with the key to Dartmoor.'
Western Daily Press

OCCULT IN THE WEST
by Michael Williams. Over 30 photographs.
Michael Williams follows his successful *Supernatural in Cornwall* with further interviews and investigations into the Occult—this time incorporating Devon. Ghosts and clairvoyancy, dreams and psychic painting, healing and hypnosis are only some of the facets of a fascinating story.
'...provides the doubters with much food for thought.'
Jean Kenzie, Tavistock Gazette

GHOSTS OF DEVON
by Peter Underwood. 44 photographs and drawings.
Peter Underwood, President of the Ghost Club, writes of the ghostly stories that saturate the County of Devon, a land full of mystery and of ghostly lore and legend.
'Packed with photographs, this is a fascinating book.'
Herald Express

SEA STORIES OF DEVON
In this companion volume to *Sea Stories of Cornwall* nine Westcountry authors recall stirring events and people from Devon's sea past. Well illustrated with old and new photographs, it is introduced by best-selling novelist E. V. Thompson.

LEGENDS OF SOMERSET
by Sally Jones. 65 photographs and drawings.
Sally Jones travels across rich legendary landscapes. Words, drawings and photographs all combine to evoke a spirit of adventure.
'On the misty lands of the Somerset Plain—as Sally Jones makes clear—history, legend and fantasy are inextricably mixed.'
Dan Lees, The Western Daily Press

VIEWS OF OLD PLYMOUTH
by Sarah Foot.
Words and old pictures combine to recall Plymouth as it once was: a reminder of those great times past and of the spirit of the people of Plymouth.
'The is a lovely nostalgia-ridden book and one which no real Plymothian will want to be without.'
James Mildren, The Western Morning News

CURIOSITIES OF DEVON
by Michael Williams.
Michael Williams explores strange and unusual aspects of a county of contrasts; curious customs and characters, strange architecture and landscapes, and highly individual Dartmoor characters. There are visits to the Finch Foundry at Sticklepath and Arlington Court.
'...a book about Devon which incorporates the essential spirit of this glorious county—individuality, diversity, yet a bond of comradeship and understanding.'
The Tavistock Gazette

MY DEVON
Ten writers writing about their Devon: Hugh Caradon, Judy Chard, Andrew Cooper, Robin Davidson, Daniel Farson, Sarah Foot, Clive Gunnell, James Mildren, Mary and Hal Price.
'...Ten writers' impressions of their favourite places...the personal approach warms and enlivens...'
Herald Express

Other Bossiney Titles

THE PLYMOUTH BLITZ
by Frank Wintle

TO TAVISTOCK GOOSIE FAIR
by Clive Gunnell

ALONG THE DART
by Judy Chard

ALONG THE LEMON
by Judy Chard

ALONG THE TEIGN
by Judy Chard

LEGENDS OF CORNWALL
by Sally Jones

DISCOVERING BODMIN MOOR
by E. V. Thompson

DISCOVERING CORNWALL's SOUTH COAST
by E. V. Thompson

GHOSTS OF CORNWALL
by Peter Underwood

STRANGE HAPPENINGS IN CORNWALL
by Michael Williams

CORNISH MYSTERIES
by Michael Williams

CORNWALL IN UPROAR
by David Mudd

KING ARTHUR COUNTRY IN CORNWALL
by Brenda Duxbury, Michael Williams and Colin Wilson

THE CORNISH COUNTRYSIDE
by Sarah Foot

AROUND GLORIOUS DEVON
by David Young

A CORNISH CAMERA
by George Ellis and Sarah Foot

GATEWAY TO CORNWALL
by Joan Rendell

THE CORNISH EDWARDIANS
by David Mudd

SEA STORIES OF CORNWALL
by Ken Duxbury

THE CRUEL CORNISH SEA
by David Mudd

CORNISH CHURCHES
by Joan Rendell

SUPERSTITION AND FOLKLORE
by Michael Williams

NORTH CORNWALL IN THE OLD DAYS
by Joan Rendell

POLDARK COUNTRY
by David Clarke

SUPERNATURAL IN CORNWALL
by Michael Williams

THE CALL OF THE WEST
by Arthur Caddick

CASTLES OF CORNWALL
by Mary and Hal Price

ECCENTRICS IN CORNWALL
by June Lander

We shall be pleased to send you our catalogue giving full details of our growing list of titles for Devon, Cornwall and Somerset and forthcoming publications.

If you have difficulty in obtaining our titles, write direct to Bossiney Books, Land's End, St Teath, Bodmin, Cornwall.